and then when the

Dan Disney

JOHN LEONARD PRESS

First published 2011 by
John Leonard Press
PO Box 443, St Kilda, VIC 3182

National Library of Australia
Cataloguing-in-Publication data:

Disney, Dan, 1970 –
and then when the

ISBN
978-0-9808523-2-5
1. Title.
A 821.4

Design: Sophie Gaur
Photo: Dan Disney
Printed and bound by BPA Print Group, Burwood, Victoria

Set in Jenson

and then when the

Dan Disney was born in 1970 in East Gippsland, where he grew up. He has worked in psychiatric institutions, paddocks, warehouses and universities, and currently divides his time between Melbourne and Seoul, where he lectures in twentieth-century poetries at Sogang University. *And then when the* is his first full-length collection.

Acknowledgements are due to editors of the following publications, where versions of some of these poems first appear: the *Age* newspaper, *Antithesis, Australian Book Review, Best Australian Poems* (UQP), *Blast, Cordite, HEAT, Island, Journal of Australian Studies, Meanjin, Overland,* and *papertiger.* Several poems first appear in a chapbook, *The Velocity of Night Falling* (Hit & Miss, 2003).

Earlier versions won the Melbourne Poets Union Prize (2001), the Somerset Poetry Prize (2004), the Broadway Poetry Prize (2006), and a Dorothy Sargent Rosenberg Prize (2010).

This book was assisted by a New Work grant from the Literature Board of the Australia Council, and by the Felix Meyer Scholarship. My thanks also to Yaddo Artists' Colony and the Tyrone Guthrie Centre, where some of these poems were written.

Special thanks to Jordie Albiston, Kevin Brophy, and John Leonard; in their own ways, each have lit paths forward. Also to the Quaglias and Maccarios, for so many things, including use of the house at Molettini, where this book was finished.

CONTENTS

. . . how strongly things exist today.

Jean-Paul Sartre, *Nausea*

Standing among the philosophy class

Coats wet, we come

fog-breathed

to hear how we might come to know the world through pure reflection

without recourse

to experience

rain on our foreheads, little fists from the *tremendum,* we wait

at the doors of an unlocked lecture hall.

Coughing has been falling from a cold man's mouth. A huddle of minds

in the dark morning

apprehend. The trees

are wearing the shape of trees.

on locating the essence of the dinner party

when coats, bottles, bouquets are thrust across night
or when guests enter bookish, miniature rooms of an apartment
shadows dissembling at the walls

when talk stumbles amid the legs of elderly chairs
when the neighbouring window's couple throw smiles
from their own dollhouse

when wine bends mirrors and laughter
(naked as candlelight) dashes for it
over the table and into the ears of everyone, welcome, or

earlier when steam curls the kitchen paint
or when there isn't conversation, just breathing, and the sparrows
who have been passing

perhaps when taxis honk in yellow, cheese vanishes
or the door claps shut with its one good hand, or is it when flowers
nod, head against stem

How to see inside machines

At least
the stars still all seem to work fine
        except of course for where the antimatter is.
In fact, with the exception of
  1. the neo-cons remastering the How-To Guide
  2. any missing space/time continuum unmoment
  3. that idiot killing the last god who worked in this thing
apart from all that
        you really do gotta love Reality.
'See you
at work church home slaughterhouse around'
        ÜBER, ÜBER, ÜBER
be careful: make it your business to know
the velocity of night falling
        'no really, there's no such thing as
a machine'
folk whisper in half light
        WE KEEP LOSING ANGELS THOUGH WE'RE NOT SURE HOW
blinking at the very idea of their hands . . . imagine, whole evenings
lit by nothing
        but *electricity*.

Vir Heroicus Sublimis

after Barnett Newman

i.

In deepsleep wards
(bedside voices are sighing 'their love of beauty
a metaphysical homesickness')
we, like moths on a pleasure flight through a bonsai forest
can hear
almost nothing.

ii.

Inside the Institute of Melancholia, test-tubes
spiral like the glassy echoes of unheard children
bright rooms filling with unopened folders marked *Whatsoever You Think*
is Illusion.
The world stays cold as a memory (breathed across a mirror).

iii.

We packed our suitcases with dirt, held our prayers, stamped
at the edges of metamorphosis: behind us
the broken city's burlesques, in front the heavy institute gates
and ether, at this height full of *gravitas.*

iv.

On the plains of this idea just beyond sight
a queue, infinitely long and not speaking, an indefinite and bloodless
transplantation.

v.

'Only such grievous ones as we
could have such godless, unspeaking gods?'

vi.

The clocks on the walls here have never once moved.

vii.

Toward a unifying theory of non-coincidence

Reality is a cliché/ From which we escape by metaphor.
Wallace Stevens *Miscellaneous Notebooks*

Late into the night we sat
practising our similes like morgue attendants in a power strike. Or an army
of amnesiacs. A draught blew
            inside a painting of a grove of trees and across, further out, a
                                    frozen lake.
No-one heard the pianos (though outside
a septet of trumpets
blew hard toward tonight
            while on TV
a philistine booted a ball to a big barbarian in shorts. The galaxy remained
happy as an underbite).
Elsewhere in the evening, in gravestone plots
            of ticking cities, the dead
(who tick not)
murmured 'we do not think; therefore we are not' while in fields
('everywhere'
            said the voice, *dolce* behind the mirror) it remained Butterflies
vs Butterfly Collectors. I remember *onceuponatime* (also
in a field big
as the world, verdant, flat) I read
            an interesting and plotless book; four cloaked guys

on muleback

the colour of a dusk newly-begun

rode out the vanishing point

              while, yes, above, a blackbird diagonal

in the empyrean

twittered on and on: 'how fragile

the promise of apocalypse, how well-wrought, how remote!'

              as the worm in its beak (I thought) shook a clenched end

                                                  at us all, yelling

'metaphor

is a cliché from which we escape by reality' while further up still

the muffled noise

              of pianos, pianos, pianos.

Smalltown études

Omeo Highway, Great Dividing Range

Bairnsdale

The sky is starling-filled granite, this open country
veneered with estates sudden as dark water rising. Main Street
                    clusters with pensioners
combing back their hair in cafeterias
and blinking over cappuccino, the *Herald Sun,* alone.
                    At the Rotunda auctioneers admire bank windows, reflective
as cattletrucks
rattling empty toward mountains.
                    Cicada husks cling to fencelines in pre-prefab paddocks.
Mares buck the abattoir scent curling at town's edge, where hammerfall
                                                                                          and lo-ing
flattens into the null.

Bruthen

Like caravans at a crossroads, the cows stand
monolithic in this quasi-primal scenery: chewing
at the floodplain trees, crooked beside roadhouses leaned back
from the horizon.

Ensay

The town clenched around its highway and roadkill, cars tilting
through the disequilibrium unstopping.
The CWA knits, and chainsaws grind at scrublines like incisors.
Somewhere (as trees fall) the ministrations of Radio National.
In the dimly-lit kitchens of farmer widows
weekly appellations
of panic: the fire brigade's
practice an occult minuet in these dry-mouthed hills
where rabbits thump the blind underground
and eels slide up pussy-willow riverbeds.
In this garden of delights it's the unquiet that is a landmark
unspoken, encircling
as the sentences of strange ghosts.

Swifts Creek

The creek bends over stone, a snake unskinning itself. Hats gather
at the servo and trucks slough past
                    unloading clear-fell at the mill. A bus draws in to school,
                                                            freckled generations
at its windows. Up the road, the cemetery
is carved with phonebook names.

Omeo

These mountains locked as a grave.
Sheep stare through seasons. Workdogs howl on chains
and fill ringbarked afternoons. Weather speculations
drawl out the half-open windows of 4WDs
in town for groceries.
Locals thumb their belt hoops. A crow scours the hills. Lawnmowers
are droning
orchestrations of dominion.

Benambra

The sky almost a void, Kosciuszko its distant steeple.
In the cleared valleys boxwood stumps gnarl
        amid haystacks inert as tractors rusting on blocks.
The weatherboards here, scant and haunted
in the bawling frames of wind, scatter out darker altitudes
        where hair-trigger farmers stark with short answers lope
                across taut daylight.
Quince and crab apple rot in dropped circles
while scarecrows mute as doppelgänger survey the wild churchyard
        long empty of its song.

Collins Street, 5pm

after John Brack

Ah, city
pylon wastelands unspooling forever-late trains, here we come

the well-born, Melbourne heigh-ho masses, amid velvety fumes
in short black everything

gangling out the quarteracre *déjà vu.*
Click go our mortgaged heels, click click click … ever since our great$^{\leq 7}$ grandfathers

slapped up tin huts and then grew a lawn
on someone else's spot, tethered their sheep

to the short, fat hills of history
(and then that austere Town Hall: on the heat-crackling horizon

sublime, or a blight?)
things have been rosier than the cheeks of a Guv'nor

jutting a gut across the swamp. Ah, Melbourne
the casino is a great place for a fight.

Look at our beloved ganglanders (now going extinct), powder-nosed and bright as
blown globes. Look at our slaphappy hoons on The Force

belting the 'ooh!' out of yobbos.
And have you seen the traffic conveyoring from unterraced suburbs

stuck fast as a glue-sniffer's nostrils?
Little wonder things get tense. Yes, Sydney

operates an Opera House but we've got the ACTU, not to mention Shane,
Wayne and Millane (RIP)

running around off their heads. When do we start shooting
bullet trains

from Warrigal. Ballarat. Geelong . . . Melburnians,
we're spread as a King Street dancer at 3am. And did you know

Burke and Wills set off from behind Parkville, that same place
Nolan-on-the-run hid, painting his Kelly series?

Why do the best *arrivistes,* arriving, leave (our huffing stencilists remain
too breathless to move away)?

Is it because the cemetery
tilts like an ill-fitting crown? Is it the dry rasp of hysteria

in our corridors of growth? Not: Howard Arkley
loved our 'burbs. Is it that we're rich as Midas, a paradise of cadavers

loping the shining streets?

How to hunt March hare

Take a gun (unloaded) to the hole one moonless night. Call your closest taxidermist friends and tell them
to stay at home. Take a portable fence on which to sit. If making noise do so politely. Wait.
Recheck your artillery. Keep waiting. Kill time with a croquet mallet and some beers.
Check the direction of the wind and your eyeballs. Wheel in a light orchestra. Grow a beard.
Kick down the portable fence. Maintain focus. Take some speed. Take some mescalin. Quote Machiavelli
through a loudspeaker from the back of a military-green shrub. Shake your fists at a god and the stars
but do not fool around with atom splitting. Build a fake hole. Climb in and imitate snoring loudly. Know your quarry well.
Help the infirm or write pornography for money. Focus. No time for waiting now. Forget your childhood nightmares
and fling a rope into the hole. Stand there with a searchlight. Hum the outro to M*A*S*H.
Annunciate loudly 'come up with your hands out!' and have the orchestra undertake an overture. Listen for the rustling
of abstraction beneath you. Rant as though there were a moon tonight. Load the gun with a paper sheet. Wait.
Pull out a cigarette. Keep waiting. Grab more beer. Looks like everyone here is in for the long haul.

Ecce hombres

A thing eats a thing
and is eaten
by another thing. This thing
not lasting long, is eaten
by a further thing
the further thing eaten by something again, eaten
soon after
by something else. This thing
is trapped and eaten by another thing
which is then eaten
by a thing. And so
it goes. This thing, kidnapped and fattened with small things
by a biggish thing
is eaten. The biggish thing-fattening thing (ambushed, carried 'twixt
a pole to a rocky place
with no garden)
is put in a stewing pot and eaten
by a thing which is eaten
by another thing eaten (soon after)
by something else. This thing is eaten by another thing called Craig.
Craig
though perhaps never believing in the unstoppable nature of destiny
is also eaten.

The eater of Craig has no name. Bored from the outset
a thing
eats the thing with no name that ate the thing that ate Craig, and is tackled
sometime later
by two other things
who pick at bones in the dark below the howled-at moon.
Later
a town of things eats a town of other things
right down to the huts and family portraits.
Soon after, a colony
of bedraggled and limping stray things
eats them as they return home but you'd expect behaviour like that from
things like those.
And so
it goes. A thing with a paunch and silver monocle
conducts a cogged factory
where things package other things
for resale in polystyrene with BBQ sauce.
Fat kahuna things
loll and burp in the gentle night in their lockdown rooms in the sky
above the canker of gutter things
being eaten
by gutter things. Dawn things

eat night things chewing dusk things on day things
swallowed by the footstepping time thing
devoured in turn by the thing-that-has-no-words thing. Wind things
eat windless things
thing things bite and gnaw at nothing things
mad screaming things suck the marrow of whisper things
and the star things eat at bits of the heavens thing.
A thing, eating a thing
becomes eaten by another thing
but
somewhere a horse made of bullion sinks to the bottom of a soundless sea
and is declared
a permanent mystery (not to mention inedible).
And so it goes.

reality is a sound, you have to tune in to

Anne Carson *Autobiography of Red*

thus we are

gigantic. We outgrow nearly ourselves.
    Did you not hear? *Sh-sh-sh!* The alarum of bells
the calibration of psyche.
    Go thither into fields of GE pigs
and robotniks
    and when you do go (close door) into that outward
try to leave quietly . . .
    everything's full of the quivers

here Superman keeps his robots, completely faithful
copies of himself

Umberto Eco *Travels in Hyperreality*

have you seen

the proliferation? We are savants
of our domain. How though do we sleep yet with the *tzzzz*
of electromagnetics? Cities so dissonant (so neo)
out from darkness marching in to the simulacrum. Blink.
Scratch. Play.
Fuck. Wake up! Pray. Stay awhile. Dystopians
we seem so real

apprehension involves no problem for it may progress to infinity

Immanuel Kant *Critique of Judgment*

everywhere

the knell of dogma! The din of knowing
    resounding in the fictions of our star-hung universe:
rocking to-and-fro *ad hominem*
    to the rulebooks of collective sanity?
And the reckoning of laws to keep the chaotic zones of us enforced
    . . . *lo!* to those who dare interrupt.
Who taught the imagination

world is a house we enter disorientated as a somnambulist

Orhan Pamuk *The Black Book*

The doorbell of every atom ringing.
        There's an orgy of sleepfulness on the landing and
a salvo of snoring in the plod-filled attic.
        Doggerel has been dribbling waxen down shirt-fronts
in the lounge; at a table of fugitive gods
        clergies are banging cutlery (necking tranqs with verve)
while we swing arms
        like so many wind-up toys

sound of their voices snapped like twigs in the air

Michel Houellebecq *Atomised*

eh?

That lo-ing from the yards? Hoist. Stun. Earplugs.
    Next. What commotion? Slit. Next!
Flossed neighbours nod polite and reach
    for a Sunday's filét roast.
Hypermart compact smiles
    over bang-arsed trolleys: a tireless grotesque plays out.
At the freezer aisle 'one must be so careful
    re the disappearance of hope' and trundling under fluorescence
toward checking out: 'it's OK' (*blip blip blip blip*) 'they don't
    even have minds'

expanse of the heavens is far greater than it appears

Plotinus *The Enneads*

ruminating

or grooming the sky? Keep your tealeaves
    to yourselves; keep the old-century stories in your heads
if you must
    but be mindful: what we cannot know we cannot

    . . . metaphysicians: heal thyselves!
Keep checking the various dimensions if your sense of limit
    keeps giving out. What's that? Static
mostly (something about prophets. Or Rael. Or Beelzebub)

and pour a torrent of light into our dark world

Mary Shelley *Frankenstein*

really? The paradigms

sh-sh-sh shifting? These are manmade days
of corporate eugenics in sunshine. Will there really come
barbarians to our gates (and what then will be standard
operating procedure)?
Meanwhile and soon there'll be requiems
to be continued: 'In tonight's news . . . *only a god can save us now*'

decay is inherent in all compound things

Buddha (dying)

once the spectacle

is switched off

every thing harkens: notice the grind of the exponential?

The mathematics of it acute as the limit and bend

of sky (oh and . . . there! Another jet

zagging horizontal into the front-teeth of a megalopolis. The

dentistry'll be mythic).

So primordial in dark suits and set truths pacing

systematic with our *Idiot's Guide to Nightmare*

toward what? And who among us invented

the *laissez-faire* of history?

Work out your own salvation. With diligence

the giving of pleasure with some useful precepts for life

Horace *Ars Poetica*

raising your eyes

unclamped and all the while seeking
    immortality? The golden means of production
enchant and then make real . . . the clangour of us imperfect
    as sensoria awaiting the succour
of authenticity. More important: beauty or its purchase? Our minds
    burn with zeitgeist while curators slink and cost-analyse
neon signs signifying 'Buy Our Thoughts
    We Make the World'. Such delectation! Gnash the gleam
of your dentures and sunglass your widened gaze. Something new will
                                                            vaunt soon
    (something always does)

Illogos

It all began with me trying to open a small wooden box
from the inside. This was a quiet place and windless too
though I left it nonetheless, kicking my way through
and into a slightly larger wooden box. Here
things were filled with a quietness and not much wind.
I kicked in the wooden wall of this box
and clambered into yet another quiet and windless box
where I thrashed the wall and took a run-up
before breaking into a slightly larger-still wooden box.
'How charmingly windless and quiet it is here,' I noted
as I kicked down the wooden wall to discover
a still slightly larger wooden box. Inside, it was windless
and quiet. As was the next wooden box, the next,
and every other box I discovered the rest of that week.

Kant's statue, Kaliningrad

. . . we must be able to view the ocean as poets do, merely in terms of what manifests itself to the eye. Immanuel Kant *Critique of Judgment*

In shade, the shopping-cart elderly glint gold teeth
sipping stale-bread beer
above a *Wehrmacht* bunker grave, one hundred thousand ghosts
in trees, in four days lost
in the Великая Отечественная Война (*'da, da! Great Patriotic War'*).[1]
How to be *a priori*
about such wilful making? This is
the Immanuel Kant State University of Russia's front lawn.

Under the lunge of airliners, of smog-dirty billboards
Kant's gaze.
'What can I know? What ought I do? What may I hope?' Five foot tall dandy
in a smock of bird shit, Kant's statue
before eternity, points beyond glasnost and cosmonauts
apartment blocks terraforming bony swamps
like a death mask.

Line 5, pron. 'Vilikaya Atyechestvennaya Vayna'

'Two things fill the mind . . . the starry heavens above me and the moral
law within me.'
The prospekts are in overdrive. An old soldier coughs and stops. Lights up
and shuffles on.
'What is a human being?' Kant's shoebuckle burnished
by wishing. An essence of crowd rumbles across dimensions, into the daytimes
of itself.
Pigeons flap. The air knocks.

Days rolled on like clockwork

This is quite generally known. Some time ago (about the time
the first star got ready to burn) it became a good idea
for fish to try and walk. Well
it was roughly that time. Soon the fish became monkeys
and some say a big flood followed. Others refute this suggestion
(I think it's a question of how you wear your hair).
To continue: it's all just a hop skip and jump from there.
Eventually we lost our tails, some thinker thought it might be nice
to make a god (and after that lots of folk tended to kill
lots of other folk, depending on the homeground advantage), cows
were discovered to be tasty, numbers and infinity
were philosophies, electricity was a thing
we could bring out of the sky, and money became the new god
worshipped by all ex-fish (only, not many found solace).
All sorts of other things happened.
The moon was walked on. Telephony got to be telepathy. Out there
the universe continued to expand. Cities did here.
Answers became products and everything discovered
got sold. Listen: they're talking about building machines that can think.
One of the things not generally known
is how much any of this matters (if at all).

Epyllion

New York, Winter

I am knocking
the table clear, skinning the room, in either hand
her rosy arse
Hell's Kitchen through the window a snowing postcard, moonlight falling
on our backs in four panes

Man with missing antithesis

. . . man is a centaur, a tangle of flesh and mind, divine inspiration and dust.
Primo Levi *The Periodic Table*

There will be mystagogues
yes and lawns mowed on weekends. There will be
a millionth bee . . . yes and a trillionth.
                And dust
and quiet desperation, multiplicity (tangled)
and soon there will be birds
with small motors (but no lightning
                from the fingertips). Verily, yes, Loris one day will be happy
as Larry.
There will be daily papers. Yes they may
read all about it.
                Flux and dark quanta
and yes
there will be sneezing
(small *faux* orgasm of the proboscis).
                There will be
coincidental hysteria, cries of *huzzah!* They will be prone
to slipping from their minds.

Yes to tennis. Yes to dictionaries. Yes to monkey wrenches.
    There will be isting
and also existing under and upon the ground.
Studies will be done
on the vagaries of monsters
    (there will be shadows the size of a crack in their days).
They will nuzzle at night
they will make pets of one another.
Here shall begin
    the vast agglomerations of *et cetera*.

. . . never come to thoughts. They come to us

Martin Heidegger *Poetry, Language, Thought*

A trapdoor has been opened in the head. Inside, historical figurines are rowing, spectred
and quaffing *logos* at the feet of mountains. See here: among them Ern Malley's shape,
toasting Plato and the Elysian mosquito swamps. In the next boat, glass to ear, Buddha,
whispering 'oh!' to a Neanderthal just returned from flower-picking in Nirvana,
where there are said to be bookshops in corridors
of infinite regress. Not much good if you can't read. The Neanderthal opens a picture book,
cloud shining from the pages, an archive of first things in unrenovated air.
Not a brassy knob or black hole out of place. Up-and-coming nature poet W. Wordsworth, seasick
as usual, peers over a prow and moans. He's neither heard of nor visited
these bookshops, yet, but half-believes it when he overhears a Cambridge shadow lament
one evening how 'the world is all that is the case!' Maybe there's a force at work,
Wordsworth thinks, a force that can open heads to screw ideas
into place. It is night as if there hasn't been a night before. Malley sighs, the wind calls, and
a shaft of moonlight tumbles through the trapdoor

across the Neanderthal's picture book, which now slams shut. Like an eye.

'These things I've seen,' said the silhouette

a play

(a man is walking down a narrow corridor. He is wearing a heavy suit and hat. The corridor is straight and has a worn floor. The man carries a torch. Footfalls echo. Yesterday he loosened his tie and broke a shoestring. Sometimes he'll cough. One of his toes is numb. The corridor continues. If he had cigarettes he'd smoke them. The man keeps walking. He doesn't sleep. There is a breeze operating according to unknown rules. The man quickens. His watch stops. A dead leaf hurries past. The man keeps walking. Floorboards creak. His footsteps are growing smaller. Nothing else happens ever. Audiences shall leave when appropriate)

Still lifes

i.m. Gianluca Lena

i.

Swallows are curving the stained weather
above worn-faced Caesars, who sweep marble arms
through the days and nights
beyond us. At the ruined Forum, the *strada*
ploughed by Mussolini for his own
idea of omnipresence.
CCTV fields of bitumen,
teenage low-grade irritants are squawking, 3D cut-outs
skateboarding across an expanse
of interesting wallpaper. Is this
the shape of us? Always stricken, homeless amid monuments,
shambling slowly as those who have travelled
such little distance
that everything seems ordinary.

Rome, 2009

ii.

The river here old vein under a skin
of afternoons. Orphan monks are pedalling
the horizon orange, beside the glimmer of machete and militia.
Factories paint the sky petrochemical. 'We keep thinking
we're a force, and keep meeting
forces stronger than ourselves,' says the professor (retired).
84 years old, her mind
a blade trained on the grammars of dead language. 'Postmodernism
was an outrage!' she jokes, sputtering
'the LANGUAGE poets use only one side of Saussure's thought/sound page'
and then a finger shakes: 'be *remembering* . . . Solzhenitsyn tells us
ideology gives evildoing its long-sought justification.' Is memory a faith,
a fatefulness? Under her sleeve, six fading numbers
won't ever fade enough.

Vientiane, 2005

iii.

A population of marble people
is milling in Westminster Abbey, gabbling the tongues of history.
Someone's left a note, 'come
Lorde Iesus, come qvicklye,' etched in stone
before rushing
into eternity. Outside, crowds of DIY men
are crossing the creative commons like Mayan acolytes to a beheading
and the afternoon begins to fit nicely
as a straitjacket. In a garden of strange flowers I'm told, 'the peal
of stillness isn't anything human,' a friend wincing
from the other side of a teacup.
Inside my head there's the scratching of wings toward a pale rim of light.
Down the road
they're selling monkey hands for voodoo.

London, 2007

iv.

Under the alabaster saints, the louche
and the wolf-faced shelter from ice storm and scowl
for caffeine. This old town
scanned by empty-roomed eyes. Where are they all? The unsound
and non-hearing, the shrill-hearted
and too-loud, prefacers and professors, the unforgotten
and not-remembered, those who read more than a third of *Purgatorio,*
the desperate and hopeful, prayerful and wilful, certain-voiced
shouting down phones at those
who believe truly
in nothing at all . . . *where are they?* All we few see are boatloads, shapes
hurrying ashore to the promise each back alley makes
where light won't go, and the rats in their slick
bed down and look on.

Genoa, 2009

v.

'The situation,' exhales
a matryoshka, dress like an Autumn night in St Petersburg,
'is excellent. We try
hard not to be numb.' Dust motes float in sun.
In this Museum
of the Great Patriotic War, light slides off
the sharp corners of propaganda
and off the shelves of Party hardhead busts. Under flags, the patriots
of Victory Square
are lynch mobs leering in sepia.
At this outpost the President is forever, blinking airspace
empty as the daylong drinking of old Soviets, windswept
as apartment blocks
howling concrete into the echelons.

Minsk, 2007

After Hermann Hesse's *Wandering*

Dear (   )

the juddering?
Nicotine and anaesthetic, a lovely time been had; one more.
Here a famous film got shot and there an empire passed, touts touting
in whatever language you are boss.
Absinthe mazurka. Snap. Snap. Snap. Under highrise afternoon
the mouth of someone
is murmuring to the ear of another someone: 'hard to see
what consciousness is from inside
the thing we're having consciousness in?' Or do we
miss the pointlessness. Sky here clapping
small dark wings over slightly monotonous fields, where sunlight has been
sinking into absence, trodden by an echo monumental as *wherefore*
now? Crags into cloudform. Architecture through haze.
Is it all some sort of orderly disaster
with trees, to think below? Hello mushroom. Between my eyes
and the heavens a golden bee is hovering, now humming, and I am asking

am I there yet? When will I be there?

Poets

as if
there's graveyard dirt on our soles, as if we live
in houses with covered mirrors, as if
each mid-morning there's no right side to climb from our beds
so many muttering about silence,
spruiking the godhead
non-descript as our job descriptions and
making memos to the immemorial
so many thinking on time, on love and where that goes, on nothing,
some days hearts may shudder

as we stoop, moan, and blink
below an audience of stars arriving early

Notes

Page 4: '*Vir Heroicus Sublimis*' responds to Barnett Newman's painting (1950-51) of the same name ❧ page 10: 'CWA' refers to the Country Women's Association of Australia ❧ page 14: '*Collins Street, 5pm*' responds to John Brack's painting (1955) of the same name ❧ pages 17-19: the refrain 'and so it goes' is from Kurt Vonnegut's *Slaughterhouse-Five* (1969) ❧ page 24: 'one must be so careful/ re the disappearance of hope' are lines from Jorie Graham's poem, 'Praying (Attempt of April 19 '04)' ❧ page 26: 'only a god can save us now' is from an interview with Martin Heidegger, posthumously published in *Der Spiegel* (1976) ❧ page 27: 'Work out your own salvation. With diligence' are reputed to be the last words spoken by Siddhartha Gautama ❧ pages 30-31: 'What can I know? What ought I do? What may I hope?' are questions asked by Immanuel Kant in his *Critique of Pure Reason* (1781). 'Two things fill the mind . . . the starry heavens above me and the moral law within me' is from his *Critique of Practical Reason* (1788) ❧ page 36: 'the world is all that is the case!' is from Ludwig Wittgenstein's treatise, *Tractatus Logico-Philosophicus* (1921) ❧ page 40: 'the peal of stillness isn't anything human' is adapted from Martin Heidegger's lecture 'Language' (1950) ❧ page 43: 'Between my eyes and the heavens a golden bee is hovering, now humming' is from Hermann Hesse's travelogue, *Wandering* (1917).

POETRY IN PRINT FROM JOHN LEONARD PRESS

2006	
A bud	Claire Gaskin
Cube Root of Book	Paul Magee
Ocean Island	Julian Croft
The Passion Paintings: Poems 1983-2006	Aileen Kelly
2007	
Vertigo | a cantata |	Jordie Albiston
The Incoming Tide	Petra White
Letters to the Tremulous Hand	Elizabeth Campbell
Man Wolf Man	L K Holt
2008	
Poems 1980-2008	Jan Owen
White Knight with Bee Box: New and Selected Poems	Peter Steele
Growing Up with Mr Menzies	John Jenkins
Therapy Like Fish: New and Selected Poems	Marcella Polain
2009	
Collected Poems	Vincent Buckley ed. Chris Wallace-Crabbe
The sonnet according to 'm'	Jordie Albiston
White camel	Morgan Yasbincek
Pilbara	Mark O'Connor
Marriage for Beginners	Catherine Bateson
2010	
The Simplified World	Petra White
Patience, Mutiny	L K Holt
Phantom Limb	David Musgrave
The Gossip and the Wine	Peter Steele
2011	
Error	Elizabeth Campbell
And then when the	Dan Disney